I Can Choose To Be Happy

By Anne "Nancy" Shriver

Illustrated by Emelia Sabine Schmidt

Edited and designed by Amabile Calvert Dyer

ISBN 978-0-934101-03-5

Published By:
Namaste Nana™
www.namastenana.com

To my grandchildren James, Olivia, Claire, and Ethan.
And with loving appreciation to Amabile, Justin,
Katherine, Vanessa, and Sue.

I am amazing!
I can do so many things!

I can
smile, I can cry,
I can laugh and be shy.
I can go see an elephant
and jump up really
high!

But, most of all...

I can choose to be happy!

Just like I can choose to be

healthy!

Happiness and health
go hand in hand,
just like...

love and kindness!

smiles and laughter!

the moon and the sun!

playing and fun!

My family makes me happy!

Thank you dad!
Thank you mom!
Thank you cousins and...

everyone!!!

I love you & you & you!

I love you!

Yes! I want to be happy!

Happiness comes from the inside first.
Inside you and inside me.
I can think happy thoughts.
I can say, "I love you," and
I can say, "thank you!"
I can say it out loud and
I can think it quietly.
I think happy thoughts because...

Thank you!

I can choose happy thoughts!

Thank you!

I love you!

I love you!

I can make a gift for my

mother

or touch someone's
heart one way or another.
I can send a letter or draw a
picture of stars in the sky.
I can write a poem about a
blueberry pie!

I can brighten up a room
with a vase full of flowers.
I can have a tea party with my

nana

for hours and hours.
Because doing kind things
for others brings me
happiness too!

Dear Ruby & Zelda,

I can daydream
about giving a tiger some of my

ice cream!

I can be kind to my friend!
Because we will be friends to the end,
through thick and thin,
frowns and grins,
day and night,
through darkness and

light!

Because..........

kindness is contagious!

Like laughter...

...and yawning!

I can wake up, smile and say...

"Good morning world!"

"May you be happy and may I be happy too!"

I can sing and dance and read.
I can see how a river flows, and
a sunbeam glows, and how a...

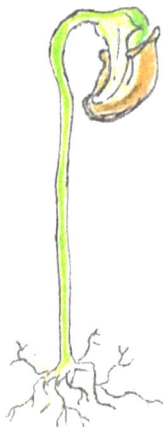

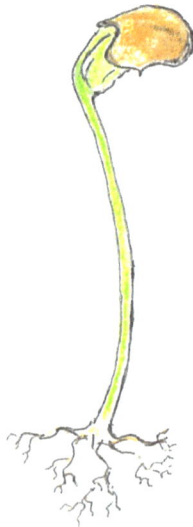

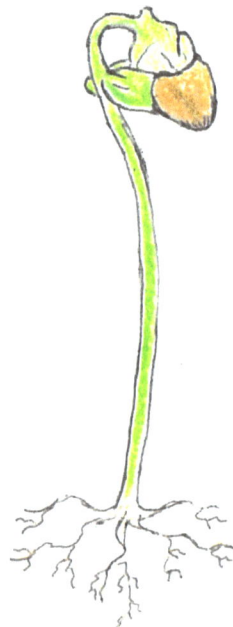

...flower grows and makes nectar for a bee!

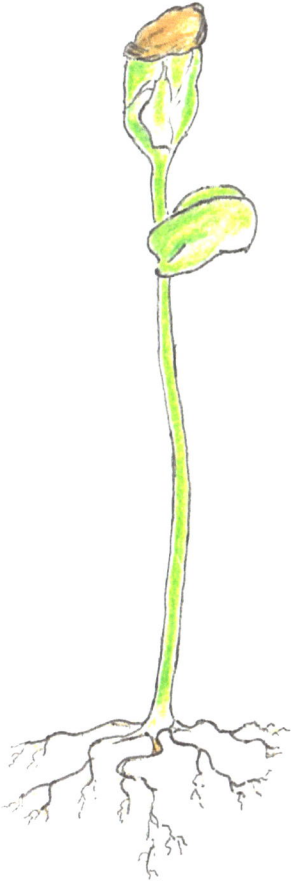

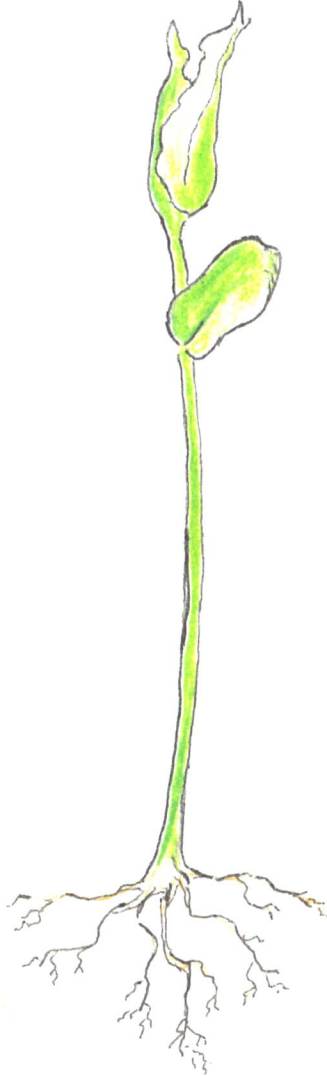

I can look up and see a dragonfly!
I can see the birdies soaring by!
I can look at a garden,
I can see the trees,
and hear the sound of the...

soft, cool

breeeeeeeeeeeeze!

There are so many ways to be happy of course!

Like pretending to ride a white winged horse!

We can fly over
mountains and
castles,
and
streams
in the land of my

brightest and wildest dreams!

I can solve a riddle,
I can play a fiddle,
I can even sing,

"Hey Diddle Diddle!"

I can choose to be happy!

I can sit still and read under a tree

Or find a secret place that is just right for me.

I can find happiness in silence and when things are quiet.

It feels really good, why don't you...

Try it!!!

When

I am happy,

it is easier to be kind to myself and

kind to everyone else!

Because sometimes things break
and don't go my way.

But these things happen and...

That's ok!!!

Because how can I be happy all the time?
Life doesn't always seem
dandy and fine!
I might feel a lump in my throat
or a pang in my belly.
My knees might get shaky
like they're made out of jelly...

Jiggle! Jiggle!
Wiggle! Wiggle!
Giggle! Giggle!

So what should I do?
Should I swim or should I sink?
Well, this is what I like to think...

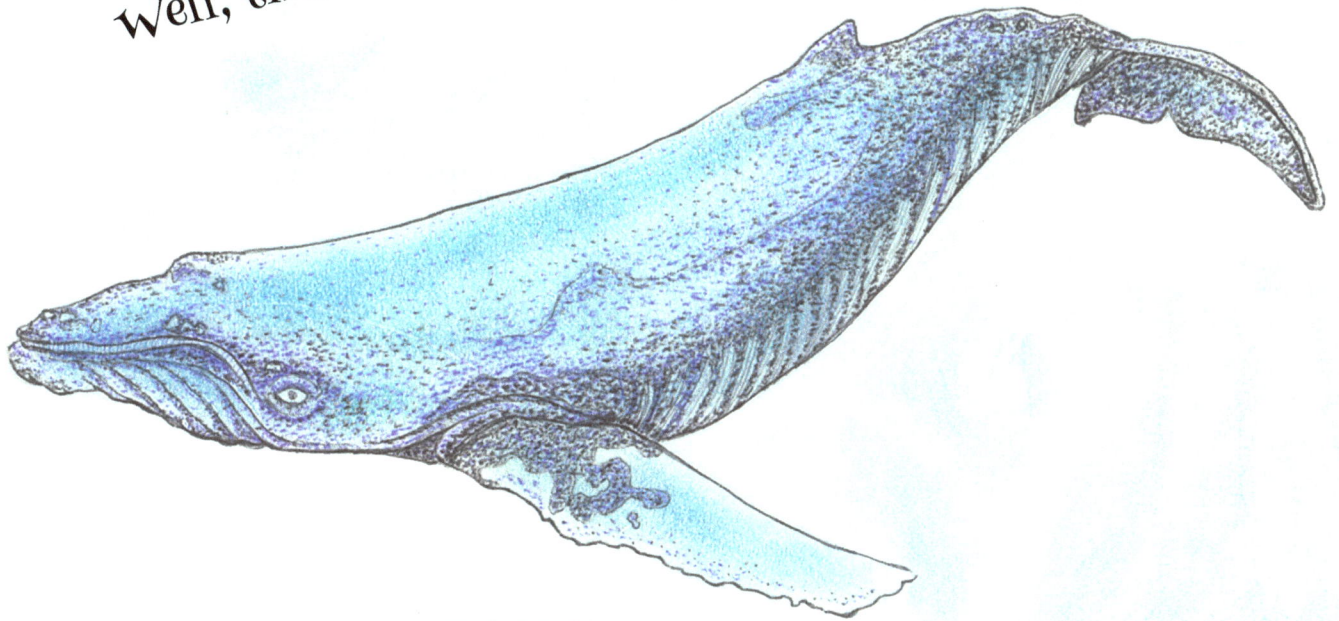

I can just let them be
for a little while,
until I find my inside smile!
I can spin 'round and around,
maybe turn upside down!
And when I jump back on my feet,
I'll come up with an idea that is

Really Sweet!!!

And then I feel good 'cuz I'm

happy again!!!

We can all choose to be...

.........happy!!!

My mind and body really want to be happy and healthy. Teenagers and grown-ups alike might learn about that in science classes. They learn about something called "homeostasis."

That is a big word that means the body and the mind want to work well together. It means if something happens, the body and the mind want to return to normal health.

"Hom-e-o-sta-sis"

A great word. Maybe you can remember it and surprise a science teacher one day!

ANNE "NANCY" SHRIVER

Nancy has worked with children for many years as a Certified Registered School Nurse. She also teaches Yoga, Tai Chi and QiGong and has personally experienced the benefits of a positive attitude and an optimistic outlook. She is very interested in sharing these benefits with others, especially with our children.

EMELIA SABINE SCHMIDT

Emelia Sabine "Beanie" Schmidt is an emerging illustration artist who also illustrated "My Body Wants to be Healthy." She grew up in Hawaii and Los Angeles, and now lives in Viroqua, Wisconsin.

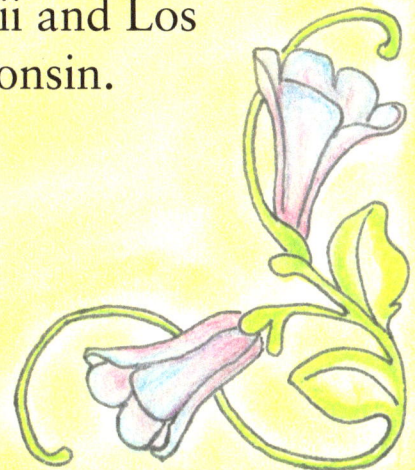

"To see each and every human being with a smile of happiness is my wish."

-Malala Yousafzai

We are happy!!!

www.ingramcontent.com/pod-product-compliance
Lightning Source LLC
Chambersburg PA
CBHW061357090426

42739CB00003B/48